I0152052

Artye W. DuLaney

JOURNEYS

of a

HEART

MIND ♥ SPIRIT ♥ SOUL

ISBN 978-0-9863672-4-3
LCCN 2016992239

Book cover and interior, design, illustrations, and layout
by Judith C. Owens-Lalude

Photographs are from the Artye DuLaney family collection

To order books
artyed1950@gmail.com
www.artyedulaney.com
and http://Amazon.com

All rights reserved. No part of this book may be reproduced in any form by
electronic or mechanical means (including photocopying, recording, or
information storage and retrieval) without permission in writing from the author
or publisher, except by a reviewer, who might include brief quotations in
a review. © Copyright 2016, Artye W. DuLaney.

Anike Press Louisville, KY 40241, www.AnikePress.com

This book is dedicated to
My parents,
Arthur and Noralee Walters,
whose loving union brought me life.
You will be forever loved and in my heart.

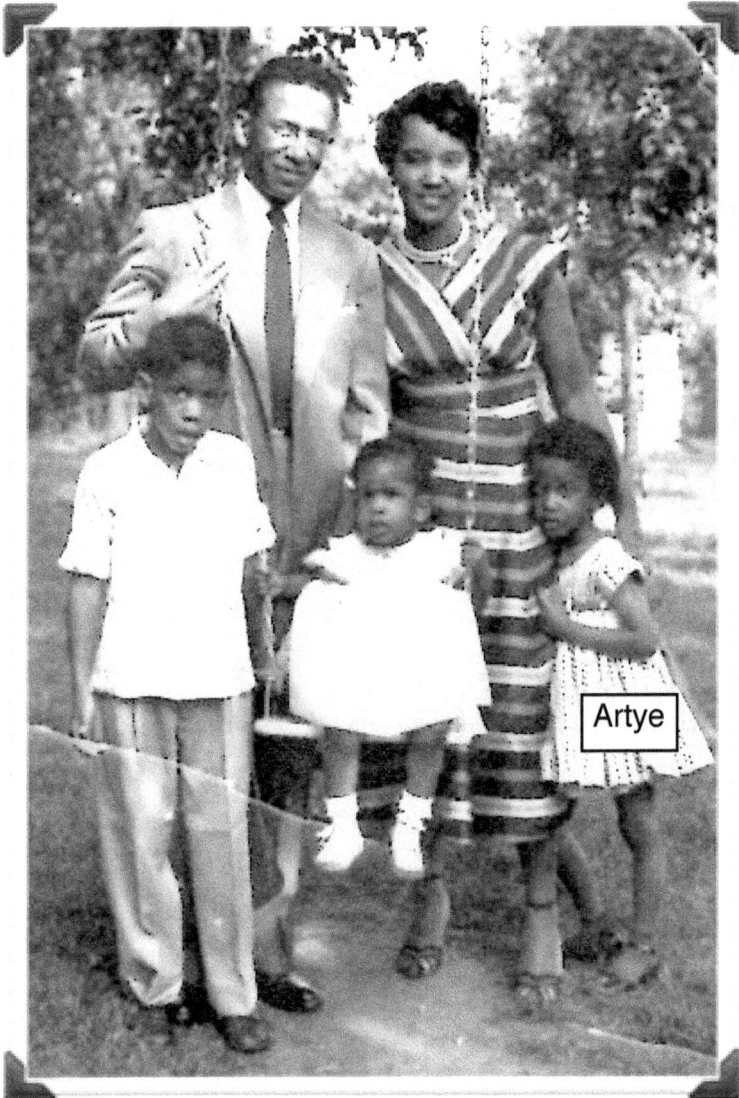

The Walters' Family, Germany
Circa 1955

Acknowledgements

First and foremost, I would like to thank God for planting in me my gifts. I would also like to thank the following:

My sister, Michele Barnett, and my daughter, Krista Bullard, for their unconditional labor of love and support in the editing of my book.

My brother, Maestro Reggie Walters, for encouraging me every day.

My brother-in-law, Randy Barnett; sister-in-law, Barbara Walters; and my awesome nieces and nephews for honoring the importance of family.

The Meredith, Walters, Carter, Board, DuLaney, and Field Families, and my church family Covenant of Faith Fellowship for their support.

A special thanks to Judith Owens-Lalude for her creative and tireless efforts in seeing my book come to fruition.

As unique creations in God's vast and wonderful universe, we will all travel various paths, yet experience different journeys along the way. It is my hope that the poems within this book will inspire and motivate you as you live from day to day.

Enjoy,
Artye

Artye at age 4

Journey
Part I

Through a Child's Eyes

Jesus is a Friend of Mine

Jesus is a friend of mine

I know this to be true

He's with me through the day and night

And I know he loves me too

He loves the flowers and the trees

And the little birds that sing

Yes, Jesus is a friend indeed

For he loves everything

So whenever I'm lonely or afraid

I can call on Jesus and say

You are my friend, I trust in you

And in my arms you will always stay

Love Is

Love is something you feel in your heart
Love is giving and sharing right from the start
Love is helping others while they are in need
Love is always doing a good deed

Love is the warmth of family and friends
Love is a special hug or grin

Love is blue skies, sunshine and rain
Love is God's light in joy and pain

Love is what God wants the world to be
Love is special, because God made you and me

Artye W. DuLaney

Mommy

Mommy, I really love you
Just want to take this time to say
Thank you for all you do for me
Each and everyday.

You're always there with open arms
To share a kind word or smile
Though sometimes you may get really tired
You always go that extra mile.

From scraped knees to little hurt feelings
You gently dry my weepy eyes
Making me feel warm and cozy again
Putting sunshine back in my life.

So all I want to do for you today
Is give you a great big hug
To the greatest Mommy in the world
FROM ME TO YOU WITH LOVE.

Written by Ms. Artye for the young ones in honor of their "Mommys"
May 9, 2004 on Mother's Day,

You Gotta Be Just Who You Are

You gotta be just who you are!
You gotta be just who you are!
Don't let nobody turn you around
Keep your head up, turn that frown to a smile
You gotta be just who you are!

Now my Jesus is the solid rock
His love is there for you and me
So if we open up our hearts and minds
We can be so free for our light to shine
And we can be all we are for Him
Yes, we can be all we are for Him!

You gotta be just who you are
You gotta be just who you are!

Now my Jesus is the solid rock
He is a friend to the great and small
If we can be who we are for Jesus
He will be right there to answer our call
And we can be all we are for Him
Yes, we can be all we are for Him

You gotta be just who you are
You gotta be just who you are
Don't let nobody turn you around
Keep your head up, turn that frown to a smile
You gotta be just who you are

Artye W. DuLaney

You gotta be just who you are

Now my Jesus is the solid rock
For my Bible says it's so true
If we can stand up tall for our Jesus
Each step we take He will see us through
And we can be all we all for Him
Yes, we can be all we are for Him…all the time!

You gotta be just who you are
You gotta be just who you are
All the time. Shining for Jesus!!

Originally written as a song for
Covenant of Faith Fellowship Youth Ministry

10-year old Artye

Journey
Part II
Growing Pains

Artye W. DuLaney

STREET CHILD

Street Child. Street Child.

Are you lost? Did you run away from home?
Or, are you alone, out on your own
trying to be grown?

It's a mean world out there.
Dog eat Dog
don't you know?

Street Child. Street Child.

If you don't find shelter, maybe some park bench will do.
Or some back alley junkie will help you make it
through the night. Yeah, good luck on that one kid!

Street Child. Street Child.

Don't think for one minute you have it all together
Just because you have some
"spare change" in your pocket
Are you saving it for a cold rainy day?
What about food? What will you do?

Street Child. Street Child.

So far away from home
What terrible deed did someone do to make you
venture into the bleak unknown?

Street Child. Street Child.

Perhaps society is to blame for the mess you're in
And although you want to be grown
your sorrowful eyes seem to yearn for help.

Street Child. Street Child.

You seem to ask
"Can anyone really feel my pain?"
And you're right, until we do
your turmoil continues.

COME HOME!

CHILDREN ARE LIFE'S GREATEST TREASURES

Children are Life's Greatest Treasures
Come whatever joy or strife
Let us be committed to encourage
Standing firm to make that sacrifice

Children are Life's Greatest Treasures
With sincere belief that their dreams will come true
May we broaden opportunities and roads to follow   A
guiding hand to see them through

Children are Life's Greatest Treasures
Let us show our patience and a smile
Yes, they *can*
reach their "highest potential"
When we strive to go that extra mile

Children are Life's Greatest Treasures
We must use our knowledge
pass it on
Instill in their hearts hope for tomorrow
Inner strength to make them strong

Children are Life's Greatest Treasures
Such jewels we hold so close and dear
Who look to us with eyes of wonder
to inspire them with words of cheer

Children are Life's Greatest Treasures
Unique and special in every way
We must lay the foundation for their future
Reflecting on experiences of yesterday

Children are Life's Greatest Treasures
whether blue skies or clouds above
For we all will be enriched with blessings
When we so graciously give them
our love

Artye W. DuLaney

IMAGES

Tell me now, what images you see
Of a child born into poverty?
Are they images of
future injustices and fears
Or of empathy, shame and sympathetic tears?

Tell me now
can we raise their hopes?
From a vicious cycle of despair
destitution, killings and dope?

Our youth are at risk
that's really the crime
It's society's albatross
Yes, yours and mine.

Tell me now
don't you think it's a pity
when plights of oppression
fall on the inner city?
For poverty knows no color at hand
It stretches ugliness throughout this land.

Tell me now, what images you see
of a child born into poverty?
Are they images of
future injustices and fears
or of empathy, shame and sympathetic tears?

UNTITLED

Reflecting childhood memories, I smile.
Playing hide and seek, running foot races,
making up dance routines.
roller skating, climbing trees with the best of them
not much to worry about,
just being a typical kid.

Reflecting childhood memories, tears fill my eyes
thinking of those children who now grow up
abused, neglected, thrown away
and misused.

Reflecting childhood memories, I smile.
always having a meal to come home to
a warm bed to snuggle in
clothes for every season.

Reflecting childhood memories, tears fill my eyes
thinking of those children who go to bed with
the pain of empty bellies
Sleeping on rotting dirt-filled floors
Tattered clothes, an everyday thing.

Reflecting childhood memories, I smile.
Role models.
Someone to look up to.
The joy of having a mom and dad.

Knowing that no matter what the problem.
they would be there to listen and care.

Reflecting childhood memories, tears fill my eyes
thinking of those children who are now raising themselves.
Gangs shouting on blood-stained streets
"Hey, home boy, we're cool. This gun is cool.
This gun means power!" And home boy listens
filling the void of wanting to belong and be loved.

Reflecting childhood memories, I smile
birthday celebrations . . . junior high school "sock hops".
Senior day.
Graduation. Plans for the future.

Reflecting childhood memories, tears fill my eyes
Thinking of a mother's anguish.
Lamenting over her child's senseless death
Another young mind wasted
Another young life…gone.

Reflecting childhood memories, I smile
Yet tears still fill my eyes.
Thinking of those children
who unfortunately are forced to
grow up
much too soon.

NOT COOL

There's nothing more disheartening
than seeing some young man sagging
Walking down the street
with his boxers exposed
Trying to hold up his trousers and dragging.
Young man! Pull your pants up.

Does it ever cross your mind
You are walking pass a grandmother, or mother?
These women you should hold in high regard
unlike any other
Young man! Pull your pants up.

Realize you're from a long line of noble kings
Who not only respected themselves
but honored and revered their queens.
Young man! Pull your pants up.

Is this the way to show the world
you're being cool?
Set an example for the little ones
and urge them to stay in school.
Young man! Pull your pants up.

So next time you hear the words,
"Dress to Impress"
No need to worry.
Your sagging and dragging will be
nowhere near passing the test.
Young man! Pull your pants up.
Sagging?
Not cool.

Artye home from college for the holidays
circa 1973

Journey
Part III

Sankofa

Bridging the Past
to the Future

A DIAMOND SO PRECIOUS

Peering up at her through
round rimmed glasses
I remember the sun shining softly on her lovely unflawed
brown complexion.

I must have been a little tyke, no more than three or four. She
held my hand
gently/ as she so often did/
She did not have to say a word
Her beautiful smile was all
I needed.

She was a soldier's wife in those early years
She wore this honor with grace.
I will always
be in awe of how she so meticulously orchestrated our many
moves across the country.
She had a knack for making sure things
were just right.

Ah, how I remember those scrumptious
"Christmastime" smells
emanating from her kitchen.
Whether it was freshly
baked cookies, cakes or pies
The aroma would seep through our nostrils

and we would seemingly just float through the air
just to get a taste of her culinary delights!

Can't leave out those memories of her home-made pizzas
and "piggies-in-a-blanket."
Now those times were truly special
Then on those cold and sometimes rainy nights
we would gather around the old RCA TV set and
watch some good old-fashioned family show
making room for interesting, warm and cozy conversations.

Mom always had quite a creative flair.
She loved to entertain in her home and instilled in her three
children the love and appreciation
of poetry, music and the arts.

I can still hear the spirit-filled gospel
sounds of Mahalia Jackson,
the unforgettable voice of Nat King Cole and the soulful
crooning of
Elvis Presley. Of course we would have our own little select
tunes with our hip-swayin'/ finger-snappin'/ not missin' a beat/
latest dance moves and mama's frequent scolding

WILL YOU KIDS PLEASE
TURN THAT MUSIC DOWN

Reminiscing

I often think of how much her expressive eyes
and assuring words
made us feel everything was going to be alright.
A mother knows the thoughts of her children.

She was a positive role model for the three of us.
Her energy, exuberance and zest for life
made us appreciate her even more through our adult years.

Yes, Mom was truly precious.
An illuminating diamond
that will always be in our hearts,
until the day when we can touch her face
and see that beautiful smile once again.
Your love will be forever felt, Mom. Love and miss you.

REFLECTIONS

Let us reflect and give thanks
for the unconditional love and
support of family and friends
throughout the year.

Let us reflect and realize
our strengths and
grow from our
shortcomings.

Let us reflect and realize that
we are on this earth for
a brief moment, and
that we should all be about caring,
lending a helping hand, cooperation and teamwork.

Let us reflect and realize
our most precious resources
are the children.
Encourage them to believe and dream
so they can reach their ultimate potential.

Let us reflect
upon those less fortunate
with hopes that they will have a chance for
better tomorrows.

Let us reflect and
give thanks for each day and
our own creativity and uniqueness
As we strive toward being
the best we can be.

HOME OF THE BRAVE
September 11, 2001

AMERICA!

Under deliberate acts of
terroristic violence
faceless cowards
invaded our friendly soil
leaving trails of
devastation, bloodshed and
innocent loss of lives.
Death came to many and
took a terrible toll a terrible toll.
Home of the Brave
Land of boundless opportunities
AMERICA!
We must now
tell our great nation to continue
in the way we have always known it to be
stoic, courageous, proud
and free
Home of the Brave
Land of boundless opportunities
AMERICA!
This was not suppose to happen
We're too sophisticated
too "high tech"

Obviously vulnerable
Having succumbed under such a vicious
senseless plan of aerial attack.
Home of the Brave
Land of boundless opportunities
AMERICA!
At what price should we
raise our weapons and
strike the enemy in defense
of our country?
All for the sake of revenge and
temporary peace?
Because it just may happen again.
Home of the Brave
Land of boundless opportunities
AMERICA!
And to our world allies
Through our hurt, our pain, our frustration our grief and our
anger
Let us unite and pray.

God Bless
AMERICA!

THOSE BEAUTIFUL SOULS

Those beautiful souls
memories of our dearly departed friends
fondly etched in the fiber of our minds
reflecting remembrances
of those once precious lives so well-loved

Those beautiful souls
just thinking of you is like witnessing the awesomeness of a
fluttering winged butterfly softly perched upon a garden rose.
In the quietness of an early morning

Those beautiful souls
We look toward the heavens and smile
And still see the illumination of your faces
as if
you never really left us
Embracing and touching our hearts, as only
those beautiful souls can do

Those beautiful, marvelous, wonderful souls will always be
cherished and held in high esteem gently tucked away in our
spirit until that day when we will all meet again

Those beautiful souls
Unlike the world so bitter and cold the warmth of their

friendship comforted us
like sipping a cup of hot cocoa by a kindling fire
on wintry nights
Yes, they truly gave us that kind of feeling
The kind of connectedness that bonded
all of us as one

What we can never forget about those beautiful souls
is how we laughed together, cried together, partied together,
protested injustices together, studied together, sang and fellow
shipped together, and shared real deep human emotions with a
kindred spirit

Those beautiful souls
while most of us can never recapture the days of our youthful
exuberance, we will always hold dear those glorious,
captivating "college days" we experienced with them

We were truly blessed to have known each of you
Who will always
and forever
be a part of us
We can take pride in knowing
You are looking down and smiling on those of us
that remain, knowing
your Heavenly Father is well pleased

Thank you for being stars in our universe and enriching our
lives and thank God for allowing such beautiful souls to cross
our journey's path. Too beautiful to be forgotten
Rest in peace beautiful souls

*On the occasion of the 7th Biennial Celebratory Reunion of the
Eastern Kentucky University African-American Alumni, humbly
paying homage to those beautiful souls who have gone before
us.*

October 2012

Artye W. DuLaney

ODE TO THE POETS OF COLOR

Our voices ring out

and echo expressions of

our proud lineages speaking from

our hearts and souls a love and

passion for the spoken and written word

Our voices ring out

reflecting on past

"freedom fighters "

Yes we,

three hundred years removed

of standing for those basic human rights

life, liberty and the pursuit of happiness

Yes we, still standing strong

Paying homage to generational wings

of grit and humility

from the ills of this society

Our voices ring out

speaking of those brave ancestors

like Harriet Tubman, Frederick Douglas and Sojourner Truth
whose spirited souls were often
tested through the fire of tough circumstances

Our voices ring out

to the place where the color of skin will be seen as something
that we just happen to be in. Embracing Dr. King's words that
content of character be the barometer
for changing racial attitudes
President Barack Hussein Obama has proven
to the American people that

Yes we can!

Our voices ring out

memories of down and out blues and making it over hurdles
and believin'
even though
that silver lining seemed so far away
Gaining strength for those sure fire journeys
that lie before us

Our voices ring out

to those special griots, Langston Hughes
and the souls of his people

Maya Angelo and the inner beauty and strength

in her powerful words

for she truly knows

why the caged bird sings

It sings for you

It sings for me

It sings for America

to take a stance for freedom

and embrace diversity

Our voices ring out

God is on our side

testimonies of His abundant love

His power His forgiveness

and His grace

giving us peace in times of the storms

and it's all because of Him that we

will continue to speak truth

CORETTA SCOTT KING
A Legacy of Faith

Throughout the night they came

human throngs abounding

Conversing in whispers

standing in silence

Young/old–black /white–rich /poor

Standing in bone-chilling temperatures

Waiting to pay their last respects to a true

Catalyst for change

She lies in gracious repose

Even in death her face reflects

an elegance and beauty

that transcends all she epitomized in life

A God-fearing woman of faith

A devoted steward

to her husband's cause

Dignitaries and Heads of State

Pay homage to her life

Her children are the fruits of a
maternal and paternal vine
upholding her legacy
keeping that faith
Knowing the price was paid
for the freedom cause
through bloodshed
and loss of innocent lives

For Freedom
as Martin would say

Is not /and will not be free
Until all people are treated
with just and dignity
To make this 21st century and beyond
A better more peaceful world
in which to live
Harmony will not only be attainable
but indeed sustainable

NELSON'S LIBERATION

Twenty-seven years of bondage
yearning to be free
they stripped you of the outside world
but not your dignity
ah sweet dignity and
that's something to be proud of

Nelson Mandela
Our Brother
Freedom

Those not yet born on your incarcerated day
lift their misted eyes to you with ecstatic jubilation they sing
"Mandela! Mandela! He'll see us through"
That's something to be proud of

Nelson Mandela
Our Brother
Freedom

A man who has patiently waited for his day
to come to past with clinched fist raised proudly toward the sky
shouting
"Oppression! It must not last.
It must not last!
That's something to be proud of

Artye W. DuLaney

Nelson Mandela
Our Brother
Freedom

That great assuring smile
Your commitment once again renewed
The struggle against apartheid
is in your blood and
that's why they believe in you
We believe in you!
and that's something to be proud of

Nelson Mandela
Our Brother
Freedom

Your liberation is part of us too

Written in celebration of Nelson Mandela's release from prison in 1990

38

WEAPONS

When we look at this great land of ours
proud flags waving from shore to shore
think of those true weapons of destruction
that have methodically eroded through America's core

For instance, those weapons of destruction
that drive people to bigotry, hatred, and strife
dehumanizing broken souls and spirits
to such a humiliating way of life

When we look at this great land of ours
with its majestic beauty of mountain and sea
think of those weapons of destruction that have emerged
from drug wars, drive-bys, and senseless killing sprees

Why do you think such weapons of destruction that occur,
from sickness of mind, homelessness and poverty
continuing to torment those painful souls
constantly yearning to be set free?

When we look at this great land of ours
beautiful beaches and spacious skies so fair
think of those weapons of destruction that arise
from sky-rocketing health costs, smog, and polluted air
Why do such weapons of destruction
take its toil on teenage
suicide, underage drinking, and pregnancy

constantly robbing our youth of their childhood
toward a better life for peace and tranquility

Yes, weapons of biological and chemical warfare
can swiftly eradicate the human race
but true underlying issues plaguing our society
can slowly put America to shame and disgrace

These weapons that we have long endured
are all part of America's plight
let's lay claim to its path of destruction
the "battle cry" is here now to get it right

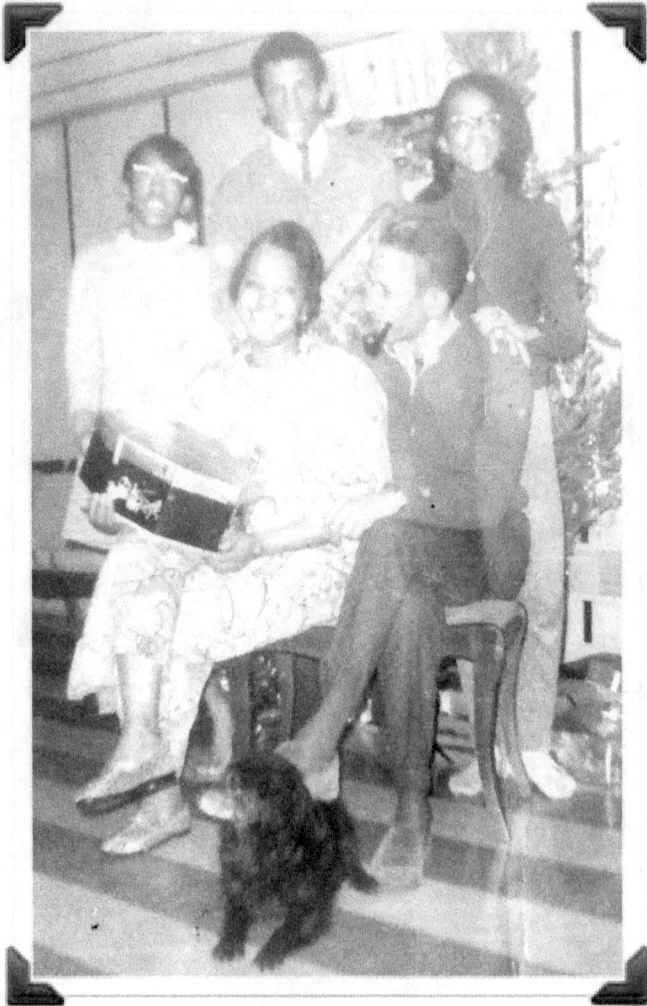

Artye, at the right, age 15
With her family

Journey
Part IV

Faith
Looking Beyond
What Our Eyes Can See

WOMANHOOD

She is a integral part of God's Divine plan
conceived from the rib of Adam
Molded and shaped to bear fruits
into miracles of life.

She is that fortified connecting link
which bonds families and nations together
Grounded in a steadfast faith
of His eternal promises.

She is a reassuring smile
a warm embrace
humbled with a heart that seeks
understanding from the Master above.

She is an advisor, aunt, author, caregiver, daughter,
doctor, entrepreneur, grandmother, mother, poet, wife, sister,
teacher, writer,

A diamond that shines when
in succinct harmony with her creator

She is peacemaker.
A mender of broken spirits.
Friend and trusted companion
Stoic, fiery, gracious, gentle, loved.

She is richly blessed and
her steps ordered by His word
Praising and lifting up His holy name
to all the world.

She is strength, wisdom and hope,
virtue, charity and forgiveness
touching the lives of many
along life's day to day journey.

She is, in essence, the salt
of God's green earth
Sprinkling flavors of her uniqueness
down through generations.

PRAISES

When you think you cannot make it
And you feel so all alone
You can have this blessed assurance
He sits high above the throne.

For He's always there to listen
And He knows our every care
All we have to do is trust in Him
And take it to Him in prayer

Just open up your heart and mind
And He will come right in
Leading us to righteousness
For He is a loyal and trusted friend.

He never sleeps or slumbers
His light shines for all to see
All the treasures of His kingdom are ours
His promise for us, eternity.

Yes, His love, forgiveness and glory
Are all part of His wonderful grace

He gives us courage to go on
Strength to run this race.

Let us give Him all the praises
For He sticks closer than a brother
Exalting Him to all the world
For above Him there is no other.

Artye W. DuLaney

THANKFUL

Each morning that I wake up
I thank the Lord above
For giving me sweet breath of life
And blessing me
with His love.

Each morning that I wake up
And see the marvel of flowers and trees
I thank God for nature's loveliness
sunshine, and gentle breeze.

Each morning that I wake up
His amazing grace I treasure
Thanking Him for His goodness and mercy
For He loves us without measure.

Each morning that I wake up
I praise and thank Him for His glory
For all His wondrous works are seen
As we tell the grand old story.

Each morning that I wake up
I thank Him for inner strength
and peace of mind

that I may open up my heart
and let my light so shine.

Each morning that I wake up
For closeness of family and friends
I thank Him for the bond of relationships
To love, to forgive, to mend.

Each morning that I wake up
I thank Him for
patience to be still.
That I may reflect upon another day
His promises to be filled.

1 Thessalonians 5:18, "In everything give thanks."

WHO ELSE BUT HE?

Who Else But He? to quiet the storms and
calm the raging sea
Who Else But He?
that we not parish
So He can set the captives free

Who Else But He?
Who brings comfort
When pain has come our way
Who Else But He?
Who always promises
to turn our midnights into day

Who Else But He?
who nurtures and heals
spirit, soul, body and mind
Who Else But He?
To gracefully forgive
just because He is so kind.

Who Else But He?
Who listens
He hears even the smallest prayer
Who Else But He? to provide a way
With assurance to always be there.

Who Else But He?
To guide our ship

when life's trials may try to prevail
Who Else But He?
to give us hope changing direction
to our sails

Who Else But He?
That we give Him honor
His glorious wonders we do amaze
Who Else But He?
That we lift Him up with esteemed reverence and praise

Who Else But He?
The King of Kings long ago a Savior born
Who Else But He?
Emmanuel sent to us on Christmas morn

Who Else But He?
He holds the world in the palm of His mighty hand
Who Else But He?
Glorious Prince of Peace
Ruler of earth heavens and land

THE WINDS OF CHANGE

Some winds can blow ever so gentle in our lives
Tapping into our minds like soft subtle breezes
Leaving shades of joy and
sunshine, hope and love.

There are times those winds come to us
like rough and sudden storms
Leaving shades of grief, sorrow, and pain to permeate our
hearts.

The Winds of Change are constant.
Nothing is going to stay the same forever
Except for the grace, mercy, and compassion
Of God's love and His sweet assuring voice
Saying "Peace. I am here and with you always."

Strange, the uncertainty of life
That allows the winds to blow our way
Like hearing the delicate whispers of silver wind chimes.
"Listen to our song" . . . they seem to say
A change is going to come.

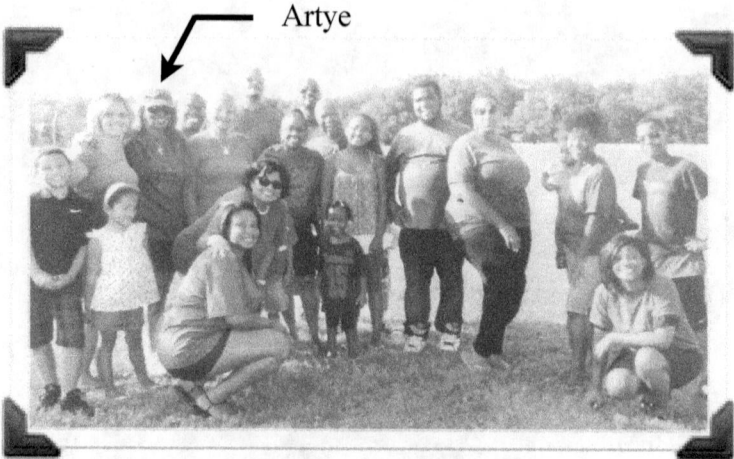

Artye

Artye and family at the
Meredith-Walters-Carter Reunion
August 2015

Journey

Part V

Family Matters

NORA AND ART
FIFTY YEARS OF LOVE

September 6, 1945
Two hearts skip a beat to say
"I Do"
bonded in love and loyalty
forever committed to be true.

He, the decorated serviceman
beaming with excitement and pride
touches the hand of his "Lady Love"
who has promised to become his bride.

Those vows they took so long ago
hold fast and strong today
Golden rings symbolizing five decades of sharing whatever joy
or strife came their way.

Through this union
there grew a family
Three little ones tugging on their mommy's dress
or jumping into their Daddy's
arms were the things they enjoyed the best.

They complement each other to the tee
and Dad has always agreed,
"Give credit to my wife who has stood by my side,
just because she believes in me."

Affectionately known as "Grand and Poppy"
by adoring grandkids
they think the world of
lending their wisdom or a listening ear
and showering them with love.

An undying faith, dedication and devotion
have inspired them through the years
for they knew
when all was said and done
there would be laughter and some tears.

As friends and family gather on this special day surely
we would be remiss, if we did not say
"Nora and Art"
Congratulations for 50 years of marital bliss.

Dedicated to Mom and Dad on their
50th Wedding Anniversary
September, 1995

CHILLIN' 1995

It's time to chill . . . and I mean
straight to the   b-o-n-e   of the matter. So
let me count the ways.

Chillin'
like giving these poor
"old dogs "a rest. After walkin'
on 'em with heels no less . . . all week long
Decked out in my professional best
upholding that image . . . to the max.

Chillin'
like wearing an old pair
of denim jeans . . . cotton shirt and barefoot no less.
Sipping a soothing cup of hot tea/slice of lemon
on the side.

Chillin'
like talkin' with family
and friends . . . reminiscing over
memories thought to be so long forgotten
Just listenin' and sharin' . . . Feelings.

Chillin'
like reading scriptures
from "The Good Book"

of a Savior's steadfast love
who died to set you and me free.

Chillin'
like really into our little girl
and her youthful exuberance
marveling over her heavy perceptions on
life . . . laughter . . . Love.

Chillin'
like on those crisp autumn days and cold winter nights
Cheering on our "hometown boys"
the Louisville Cards all the way!

Chillin'
like relaxin' on a laid-back afternoon
Enjoying soulful mellow sounds of those wonderful
Oldies but Goodies
Marvin, Aretha, The " temptin' " Temptations, Stevie, and Smokey.
Yes indeed, the great Motown Sound 101.3 on your radio dial.
Sure don't make' em like they use to, do they?

Chillin'
like writing from within this
heart and soul and mind and being
my poems.

A PIECE OF CHRISTMAS

Pass along a piece of Christmas
As we live from day to day
Share a smile or warm embrace
Encourage someone along the way.

Pass along a piece of Christmas
To the homeless and needy of this world
Giving of our time and special talents
To some precious boy or girl.

Pass along a piece of Christmas
Perhaps the gift of "love" to start
For we can feel good within ourselves
When we are giving from the heart.

Pass along a piece of Christmas
Down this smooth and rocky road called "life"
Whether it be tears, sorrow, grief or pain
You can see joy through the strife.

Pass along a piece of Christmas
Be it neighbor or a friend
Let the light within us shine
From dawn to evenings end.

Pass along a piece of Christmas

Spreading true goodwill and cheer

Not only at Christmas time

But "peace" throughout the year.

May the true meaning of Christmas

bring you peace

happiness

and

God's blessings.

WHAT MAKES A FAMILY?

What makes a family is the strength
of commitment hope and care
Taking the joy and the pain striving to
always be there.

What makes a family is the faith
of God's assuring plan
Knowing we can lay our trust in Him
He's always there to take our hand.

What makes a family are the smiles
some familiar or friendly face
Being there in your time of need
with a kind word or warm embrace.

What makes a family are lessons learned
from kinship living and gone
Admiring remnants of that "family tree"
through pictures, old stories or songs.

What makes a family are special occasions
graduations, anniversaries, a new birth

Milestones that touch those hearts and souls
with great humbleness and mirth.
What makes a family are the children
instilling in them these jewels
A caring spirit, respect and love of self
qualities for the golden rule.

What makes a family is communication
a way of talking things out
Expressing those thoughts and concerns
Is what a family's about.

What makes a family is the wisdom
those loved ones with seasoned years
"Listen to the elders" they often say
They can guide you through the tears.

What makes a family are daily blessings
When giving thanks to the Lord above
What makes a family are all of these things
But that one special ingredient is love.

IN CELEBRATION OF FAMILY

IN CELEBRATION OF FAMILY
God's blessings, grace and love in times of
sunshine and rain. Feeling the warmth
of his steadfast arms, protecting us
in every way.

IN CELEBRATION OF FAMILY
Holding a little one's hand. Guiding, sharing,
molding a life, bonding . . . bloodlines
It makes a family grow

IN CELEBRATION OF FAMILY
Uplift a broken spirit. Lighten a heavy
load. Renew a kindred soul.

IN CELEBRATION OF FAMILY
Friendship over troubled times
Laughter,
a sincere smile
yes, unconditional love.

IN CELEBRATION OF FAMILY
Self-Esteem. Respect for others.
Commitment to be the best we can be.

IN CELEBRATION OF FAMILY
Growing in acceptance of our own uniqueness.
and possessing that faith which unites us.

IN CELEBRATION OF FAMILY
Reflecting on the wisdom of our elders
down through the years. Inspiring
us to move on with courage and
determination.

IN CELEBRATION OF FAMILY
Reach out to feel
and touch human emotions
Pulling together on one accord.

IN CELEBRATION OF FAMILY
With affirmation, unity and trust
let us continue to be about love
making the difference for us to keep on
Keeping on.

FAMILY IS A FOREVER PLACE

Family is a *forever place*
A beautiful life begins
and unconditional love never ends
Family is a chid's first circle of friends.

Family is a *forever place*
with trust of a mother, father, sister, brother, aunt, uncle,
grandfather or grandmother
It's where you fit in and truly belong
By caring for one another.

Family is a *forever place*
encouraging, reminiscing and embracing
it's finding ways of letting go
from hardships you may be facing.

Family is a *forever place*
where "life lessons" are taught and learned. Gaining wisdom
from the elders down through the years of ways we can grow
and discern.

Family is a *forever place*
We come in all shapes, sizes and personalities
Some are laid-back, some are high-strung

but the bottom line is
we are in this bond together
for we are as one.

Family is a *forever place*
Like flourishing branches on a beautiful tree
We spread our wings
We laugh, we cry, we frown, we sing, we disagree, we agree,
we go beyond what our eyes can see.

Family is a *forever place*
and being thankful
For each new day
It's sitting at the family table
and taking time to pray.

Family is a *forever place*
A smile, a hug, a spirited conversation, a gentle
touch, these things we hold so close
and dear can mean so very much.

Family is a *forever place*
Celebrating milestones big or small
birthdays, weddings, reunions, graduations
and praising God through it all.

Family is a *forever place*
Where we seek peace of mind, tranquility and an honest living
A place of mutual respect
Where we are always giving.

Family is a *forever place*
For God has kept us in the midst of it all
As we continue to keep the faith
we can hold our heads up
and be strong.

Family is a *forever place*
where we hope, we dare, we dream
Family is togetherness, strength, courage and love
For we are all on the same team.

Dedicated to the Walters-Meredith-Carter Reunion 2015

A MOTHER'S LOVE IS ALWAYS THERE

A newborn baby cries
trembling for the warmth
and security of her mother's womb
She caresses her little one
that she holds so dear
A Mother's Love Is Always There.

A toddler tugs tightly on his Mother's dress
making sure she does not stray
too far away from his trusting eyes
She tells her little one
"Mommy's here."
as she lifts him high into the air
A Mother's Love Is Always There.

The long yellow bus rolls down the road
The child jumps up and down so full of glee
Wow, his very first day of school!
She wonders how fast the years have flown
As she prepares a backpack with loving care
A Mother's Love Is Always There.

Adolescent years. Seeking their own self-identity.
She looks at Mom in a different light
"I'm not a little kid anymore, Mom!"
And you know she's not.

Artye W. DuLaney

Not grown either/ Guidance/ Tough love advice
Lighten up on those apron strings if you dare
A Mother's Love Is Always There.

Made it through those "wonder years"
Graduation day fast approaching
Her eyes glisten with tears of pride
Reminiscing of the joy and the pain
Knowing God knew how much she could bear
A Mother's Love Is Always There.

Down the path of life's highway
A young adult dreams of tomorrows ahead
What will the future bring? /College? /Marriage?
Perhaps a tiny new life?
Whether the road is rugged or fair
A Mother's Love Is Always There.

These are milestones that touch a maternal heart
With tender loving care
A Mother's love is a deep-rooted love
Yes, a Mother's Love Is Always There.

MOTHER

A Mother's Love
can mend a hurt
or dry a tearful eye
Her beauty shines so brightly
like stars upon a night sky.

A Mother's Love
grows strong in faith
through grace and daily prayer
She holds her family in high esteem
Always willing to give and share.

A Mother's Love
can be like a storm
or a gentle blowing breeze
She finds it in her heart to forgive
Through circumstances of pain and ease.

A Mother's Love is a radiant smile
or even a warm embrace. She gives encouragement to go on
Strength to run this race.

A Mother's Love
sacrifices and nurtures
Yes, her children are her pride and joy
Giving advice or a listening ear
To a little girl or boy.

A Mother's Love
is that strong belief
that God holds the "Master Plan"
Putting her care and trust in Him
Holding to His unchanging hand.

A Mother's Love
is but a memory
Some have gone the last mile of the way
But if we do right on this lowly earth
We will see her again one day.

A SPECIAL SOMEONE

It takes a special someone, who will stand
by his children through the years. That special
someone standing tall
sharing triumphs, laughter and tears.

It takes a special "Man Who Cares" to reach out
to those in need. Giving so graciously
of himself without animosity or greed.

It takes a special someone, who gives day by day
"true love". With commitment and belief
he places everything in
his creator above.

It takes a special someone, who may not outwardly
show his emotions
but "still waters run deep,"
and just by doing
is a measure of his devotion.

It takes a special someone
who believes in three precious jewels
respect for others, a love of self
and follow the golden rule.

It takes a special "man of faith" to appreciate
the sunshine and rain
A man who believes that
through it all
he will persevere in times of pain.

It takes a special someone
who possesses courage
whether situations are happy or sad
It's true that a man can father children
But it takes a special someone to be a Dad.

A dedication poem to those
special men who have made the difference

A LOVING FATHER

A loving father encourages and guides
And everyday shows his love
To everyone who is blessed to be around him
They witness his faith
In his heavenly Father above

A loving father is patient and kind
Provider, helpful, gentle and strong
He is someone who listens yet
gives stern advice to young folks who
May try to go wrong

A loving father answers to many names
Hubby, Dad, Daddy, Poppy, Uncle, Brother,
Granddaddy, and Friend
A humble heart that brings happiness to others
He's someone who you can depend

A Loving father's character cannot be measured
By his status, physical strength or girth
for God looks on the inside of his soul
Determining his true value and worth

Some loving fathers have gone on to glory
Precious memories their loved ones impart
Just knowing they are resting in God's
loving arms

Brings peace and solace to their hearts
To all our loving fathers who bring us joy
To those both far and near
Just remember how much
You are admired and loved
Today and throughout the year

"Hear ye children, the instructions of a father and attend to know understanding"

Proverbs 4:1

Dedicated to my father, Arthur M. Walters

Artye and granddaughter, 4-year old Kaelyn

A GRANDDAUGHTER IS LOVE

She is four now
Inquisitive, funny and full of glee
It's such a joy spending time with her
She loves spending time with me.

I love to hear her laugh
Her smile lights up a room
Her exuberance and energy is non-stop
When you are with her
You just can't feel gloom.

I Spy I Spy With My Magical Eye
a game we like to play
naming all colors of the rainbow
As we hold hands along the way.

She's smart, creative and has a musical ear
and to her family she means the world
Yes, Kaelyn is a real sweetheart and
Granna's precious little girl.

. . . and the journey continues

Journey
Part VI

The Present
A Gift

Artye W. DuLaney

BIRTH OF A POEM

It might first be conceived
as a certain thought
your mind
in a serious vein or
it just might begin
on a whimsical note
For no particular gain

It could start from your
own experience
Some chapter in your life or
center on some poor lost soul
Who has given up the fight

With pen in hand
you express these thoughts
through verse or
unrhymed lines
you see it all fall into place
when the words are well defined

After all this is done
from conception to end
The greatest joy I'll find
is seeing someone's smiling face
after hearing a poem of mine

Taken from the poetry book
EXPRESSIONS by Artye DuLaney

A PLACE TO CALL HOME

The crowdedness of a shelter
The loneliness of the streets
Impoverished
families struggling along
Just trying to make ends meet.

In hotels, motels or on scattered campgrounds
a child stares at the stars shining bright
Wonders of pipe dreams fill his thoughts
in the stillness of the night.

Young people wandering aimlessly suddenly
out there on their own
Desperately seeking a refuge
to anywhere that they may call home.

A young mother bends down
with a tear in her eye
gently caressing her little one
yet refusing to cry.

Life's hard knocks and scratches cannot ease the pain
From years of abandonment
sickness and shame.

Sleeping on public corners and in tight little spaces
Their eyes search for smiles
from expressionless faces.

To maintain one's dignity and
some semblance of pride are
true measures of courage in
the midst of the tide.

The homeless have rights
just like you and me
and when given a chance
They, too, can believe.

Yes, we should open our hearts
with compassion and care
that whatever the circumstances
advocates for homeless families
children and youth will be there.

TIME

Tick Tock Tick Tock, Time.
Where did it go? I don't know.
I need more time. Time to grow.

Maybe next time. The time is now.
What time is it? I gotta run.
Take time for family and friends.
Hey, take time to have fun.

Time is of the essence.
Keep time with the beat.
Time for victory.
Sometimes defeat.

In the nick of time. The times of our lives.
A time to be born. Inevitably, a time to die.
Ecclesiastically speaking, there's a time for every
purpose under the heavens.

Or thinking of an old song with its familiar rhyme
"If I could turn back the hands of time"

I remember when the old folks use to say,
"Honey you betta look to that
private closet,
drop on your knees and take time to pray"

You see, time is always slipping away.
So, have you taken the time to
encourage someone today?

Do you think time is really on our side?
We better get our houses in order
Treat others right and take life in stride.

Tick Tock Tick Tock.
Like the steady rhythmic motions of a river's flow.
Time just keeps on rolling along.
Tick Tock Tick Tock
Time.

A ROSE

A Rose is full of marvelous wonder
and everlasting grace
It radiates true warmth and affection
that can brighten up a face.

A Rose is like a innocent child
nurturing hands can make it bloom
It gives us strength and comfort
when we walk into a room.

A Rose can mend a hurtful heart
with tender loving care
Its beauty shines for all to see
reminding us to share.

A Rose is like a special friendship
that has endured down through the years
Just a simple solitary reminder
to take the good times and the tears.

A Rose is like a gentle breeze
Calming those uncertain days ahead
A wonderful miracle to behold
giving hope, instead of dread.

A Rose is like that special someone
that you think the whole world of
A Rose is a symbol of God's pride and joy
Yes, a Rose is a blessing of love.

A SMALL FIBER OF OURSELVES

All it takes is one small fiber
a little 'giving of ourselves'
Celebrating our unique differences
not measuring class or wealth.

All it takes is one small fiber
whatever our station in life
That beliefs and opinions be freely expressed
without the pain of humiliation or strife.

All it takes is one small fiber
looking at humanity face to face
Tearing down those barriers of discrimination
across all disabilities, religion, gender and race.

Unity, commitment and community support
are small fibers that will withstand the test
For through it all, we've got to believe
that 'peace' will do the rest.

All it takes is one small fiber
through hope, may our children see our strength
Instilling in them a 'true love of self'
a precious jewel, at any length.

All it takes is one small fiber
empowerment to find a way
For people of all colors, must trust and understand
if we are to make a change today.

Affirming those things we hold most dear
not tolerating abuse or neglect
Are small fibers that will truly enlighten us
to treat people with dignity and respect.

All it takes is one small fiber
and this we all should know
"Educating this nation" is essential
for society to prosper and grow.

Yes, embracing our own uniqueness
through cooperation, harmony and care
Are fibers that can be molded and
shaped in this world
when we take a stance to dream and dare.

IT'S IN YOUR HANDS

It's in your hands "the knowledge key"
that must unlock curious minds
Young minds that love to seek and learn
bright minds that yearn to strive.

It's in your hands "the knowledge key"
that builds up self-esteem
Encouraging, motivating, giving of your time
so that "every" child may dare to dream.

It's in your hands-and with that key
be determined to give them your best
With leadership, inspiration and fortitude
These qualities will withstand the test.

It's in your hands to mold and shape
your program of success
For teaching is still a noble cause
one notch above the rest.

It's in your hands empowerment to motivate
the child who has lost his way
Offering insight, wisdom, guidance and love
for future brighter days.

It's in your hands
the key that will elevate
your special field to soaring heights
With innovation and a renewed sense of hope
this will surely come to light.

Yes, your hands hold the key to their potential
keep that vision always in mind
With commitment and dedication, those goals
can be reached
across the realms of time

KENTUCKY SUNSHINE

Somehow the beauty of Kentucky's sun seems to
radiate down with a brilliance
unlike any other

It spreads its rays
through the blustering trees
as the wind whistles its breath
through every flowing leaf

Its reflection shines on lakes and rivers
and descends with a brightness
over valley peaks

It looks down on glittering bluegrass
after the rain
as the thoroughbreds and colts
graze and romp

And
as evening approaches
while nestling its huge circumference
behind some distant hill
it slumbers,
awaiting next days dawning.

Taken from the poetry book
EXPRESSIONS by Artye DuLaney

In memory of my husband, Darryl DuLaney
and my grandson, Kameron Bullard,
resting in the cradle of God's arms.

About the Author

Artye W. DuLaney, a graduate of Eastern Kentucky University, retired in 2013 from the Kentucky Department of Education after a 30-year career. She was a guest author in the annual Kentucky Book Fair (1989) and participated in an Arts and Poetry Festival at the Kentucky Center for the Arts (1996). Her works have been published in "The Storytellers", an arts and humanities publication of the African American Women's Literary Series (1996), The Louisville Defender's Newspaper (1997), and poetry anthologies, Theater of the Mind and Eternal Portraits (2003 and 2005). Other accolades have included recognition for High Achievement in the Arts from the City of Louisville's Metro Parks Poetry contest (2003). Most recently, she received first place honors in the Writing for Children & Teens contest (2013). *Journeys of a Heart* is her 2nd book of poems. The first book, *EXPRESSIONS,* was published in 1989.

Artye resides in Louisville, KY. ***Journeys of a Heart: Mind, Spirit, and Soul,*** is a diverse collection of poems which highlights her life experiences that will resonate with everyone.

www.ingramcontent.com/pod-product-compliance
Lightning Source LLC
LaVergne TN
LVHW021540080426
835509LV00019B/2759